BELIZE 2016 HUMAN RIGHTS REPORT

EXECUTIVE SUMMARY

Belize is a constitutional parliamentary democracy. In November 2015 the United Democratic Party (UDP) won 19 of 31 seats in the House of Representatives following generally free and fair multiparty elections. Civilian authorities maintained effective control over the security forces.

The most important human rights abuses included the use of excessive force by security forces (especially the police), lengthy pretrial detention, and harassment and threats based on sexual orientation or gender identity.

Other human rights problems included corruption by government agents, lack of protection of refugees, domestic violence, discrimination against women, sexual abuse of children, trafficking in persons, and child labor.

In some cases the government took steps to prosecute public officials who committed abuses, both administratively and through the courts, but there were few successful prosecutions. While some lower ranking officials faced disciplinary action and/or criminal charges, higher-ranking officials were less likely to face punishment, resulting in a perception of impunity.

Section 1. Respect for the Integrity of the Person, Including Freedom from:

a. Arbitrary Deprivation of Life and other Unlawful or Politically Motivated Killings

There was one allegation that government agents committed an arbitrary or unlawful killing. Three police officers in San Pedro Town were initially charged with murder after they allegedly beat 30-year-old Edwin Ixpatac to death in March. According to the police report, two police officers responded to reports that Ixpatac had been drinking at a bar and was acting in a disorderly manner, and they found him injured. Police did not seek medical attention for him and detained him until the following morning, when authorities realized he was unconscious in his cell. Video footage showed he was abused by three officers, and the post mortem revealed that he died from a blow to the head, which investigators claimed he received during his detention. The Belize Police Department (BPD) admitted administrative neglect on the part of the officer in command but stated police authorities would deal with it internally. In October the Director of Public

Prosecution downgraded the charges against the three officers from murder to manslaughter, and the men were released on bail awaiting trial.

b. Disappearance

There were no reports of politically motivated disappearances during the year.

In August 2015 three Belize City fishermen went missing while at sea. Family members claimed members of the Belize Coast Guard were involved in the disappearance of the men. A police investigation resulted in the detention of three members of the Coast Guard. There were no reports of further developments in the case.

c. Torture and Other Cruel, Inhuman, or Degrading Treatment or Punishment

The constitution prohibits torture or other inhuman punishment. There were reports that police used excessive force, and there were other allegations of abuse by security force personnel.

The government occasionally ignored reports of police abuse, delayed action, failed to take disciplinary action, or transferred accused officers to other areas within their department.

The Ombudsman's Office stated that it received 217 new complaints of police abuse in 2015 and that 41 percent of these were either investigated, resolved, or under investigation. Police abuse was the most common complaint, in particular against members of the Gang Suppression Unit. The Office of the Ombudsman also noted an increase in complaints against the Immigration and Nationality Department. The BPD's Professional Standards Branch (PSB) received complaints from all parts of the country, but the majority were from Belize City.

In one example an alleged victim from the Toledo District stated that police officers beat him when he intervened while police were attacking another individual. The alleged victim said that he was left on the roadside, where he was found the following day suffering from internal injuries. Members of the victim's family claimed that when they approached the PSB with their complaints, the officers delayed in dealing with the matter. As of October the BPD had not acted on the matter.

Prison and Detention Center Conditions

Prison conditions did not meet all international standards. The Kolbe Foundation, a local Christian nonprofit organization, administered the country's only central prison, but the government retained oversight and monitoring responsibility.

Physical Conditions: Prison officials held women and men in separate facilities. Conditions in the women's area were significantly better than in the men's compound. Officials used isolation in a small, unlit, unventilated punishment cell, called a "reflection room," to discipline inmates.

There were no reported cases of officers abusing their power. During the year, however, prison authorities investigated seven cases of inmate-on-inmate assault involving "gross violence." Because inmates were generally not willing to press criminal charges against their attackers, the prison's internal tribunal system handled all cases. Penalties included temporary segregation or temporary suspension of privileges, depending on the severity of the assault.

Administration: Despite the fact that the law authorizes inmates to make complaints to the Ombudsman's Office only through prison authorities, inmates (and sometimes their family members) continued to make complaints directly to the ombudsman, who could not fully investigate complaints. The prison administrator's chief of security initially investigates allegations of excessive use of force. If the investigation discovers incriminating evidence, the accused officer is disciplined. If there is evidence of officer corruption, the investigation is passed to the administrator's intelligence officer, who further investigates the matter.

Independent Monitoring: The prison administrator permitted visits from independent human rights observers, and, while the prison generally operated free from government interference, the Ministry of Home Affairs monitored it on site through the Office of Controller of Prisons. Observers had access to the prison grounds and could visit inmates.

d. Arbitrary Arrest or Detention

While the constitution and law prohibit arbitrary arrest and detention, there were several allegations made through the media and to the PSB that the government failed to observe these prohibitions. In addition, due to substantial delays and a backlog of cases in the justice system, the courts in some cases did not bring minors to trial until they reached 18 years; in such cases the defendants were tried as minors.

Role of the Police and Security Apparatus

In July the government divided the Ministry of National Security (which oversaw the police, prison, and military) into the Ministry of Home Affairs (police and prison) and the Ministry of Defense (military). Although primarily charged with external security, the Belize Defense Force (BDF) also provides limited domestic security support to civilian authorities and has limited powers of arrest.

There were reports of impunity involving the security forces, including reports of police brutality and corruption (extortion cases primarily). The PSB investigates complaints against police, including regular officers, civilian police, and special constables. An assistant commissioner of police, supported by seven officers, heads the PSB. The law authorizes the police commissioner to place police personnel on suspension or interdiction (a modified suspension with lesser penalties if the case is still under investigation). As of October the PSB received 64 formal complaints of alleged severe police misconduct. The PSB reported 41 officers were on interdiction or on suspension, of which 16 suspensions took place during the year. Additionally, authorities use police investigations, coroner inquests, and the Director of the Public Prosecutions Office to evaluate allegations against police.

In April members of the BDF and a group of forest rangers on patrol near the border with Guatemala were involved in a shooting incident with Guatemalan civilians in which a Guatemalan minor was shot and killed. An Organization of American States (OAS) investigation revealed that the child's injuries came from a firearm belonging to the forest rangers and that the Guatemalans had fired on the Belizean officials.

In August, two brothers accused the Gang Suppression Unit of shooting them both in the leg while in detention following a raid by the unit on an area well known for gang activity in Belize City. An investigation into the shooting was pending.

Arrest Procedures and Treatment of Detainees

Police must obtain search or arrest warrants issued by a magistrate, except in cases of hot pursuit, when there is probable cause, or when the presence of a firearm is suspected. Police must inform a detainee of his rights at the time of arrest and of the cause of his detention within 48 hours of arrest. Police must also bring a detainee before a magistrate to be charged officially within 48 hours. The BPD faced allegations that its members arbitrarily detained persons beyond 48 hours without charge, did not take detainees to a police station in the required manner, and used detention as a means of intimidation.

The law requires police to follow the Judges' Rules, a code of conduct governing police interaction with arrested persons. Although judges sometimes dismissed cases that involved violations of these rules, they more commonly deemed confessions obtained through violation of the rules to be invalid. Police usually granted detainees timely access to family members and lawyers, although there were occasional complaints from detainees that authorities denied a telephone call after arrest.

By law a police officer in charge of a station may grant bail to persons charged with minor offenses, but those charged with more serious crimes--including murder, gang activity, possession of an unlicensed firearm, and specified drug trafficking or sexual offenses--must apply to the Supreme Court for bail. The Supreme Court reviews the application within 10 working days.

Pretrial Detention: Lengthy trial backlogs remained, particularly for serious crimes such as murder. As of December 14, there were 528 persons on remand at the Belize Central Prison. Approximately 182 persons were awaiting trial at the Supreme Court, predominantly on homicide charges. Problems included police delays in completing their investigations, investigative follow-up, court delays in preparing depositions, and adjournments in the courts.

Judges occasionally were slow to issue rulings, in some cases taking a year or longer. The time lag between arrests, trials, and convictions ranged from six months to four years and in some cases up to seven years. Pretrial detention for persons accused of murder averaged three to four years.

Detainee's Ability to Challenge Lawfulness of Detention before a Court: Persons arrested or detained, regardless of whether on criminal or other grounds, are entitled to challenge in court the legal basis or arbitrary nature of their detention and obtain prompt release and compensation if found to have been unlawfully detained.

e. Denial of Fair Public Trial

The constitution provides for an independent judiciary, and the government generally respected judicial independence.

Trial Procedures

The law provides for the right to a fair public trial, and an independent judiciary generally enforced this right, although delays in holding trials occurred. A magistrate generally issued decisions and judgments for lesser crimes after deliberating on the arguments presented by the prosecution and defense.

The law stipulates that nonjury trials are mandatory in cases involving charges of murder, attempted murder, abetment of murder, and conspiracy to commit murder. Government officials stated that this law protects jurors from retribution. A single Supreme Court judge hears these cases.

Defendants enjoy a presumption of innocence and have the right to defense by counsel and appeal. The court has the authority to exclude defendants from the courtroom if it determines that the opposing party has a substantiated fear for his/her safety, in which case the court can grant interim provisions that both parties be addressed individually.

There is no requirement for defendants to have legal representation except in cases involving murder. The Supreme Court's registrar has the responsibility of appointing an attorney to act on behalf of indigent defendants charged with murder. In lesser cases the court does not provide defendants an attorney, and defendants sometimes represented themselves rather than hire an attorney. The Legal Advice and Services Center, staffed by three attorneys, can provide legal services and representation for a range of civil and criminal cases, including cases of domestic violence and criminal cases up to attempted murder. Defendants are entitled to adequate time and facilities to prepare a defense or request an adjournment, often used by the defense as a delaying tactic. Defendants may not be compelled to testify against themselves or confess guilt. Defendants have the right to appeal their sentences to a higher court and the right to free interpretation as necessary from the moment charged through all appeals.

The law allows defendants to confront and question witnesses against them and present witnesses on their behalf, but written statements by witnesses may be admitted into evidence in place of court appearances. Judges generally admitted a statement if it was complemented by other evidence pointing to the defendant's guilt, but they were sometimes reluctant to admit witness statements without the presence of the witness at the trial if it was the sole or main evidence suggesting guilt. The law allows the prosecution to submit the content of previous testimony as official statements when the witness is a hostile witness. Judges remained reluctant, however, to take this step. Judges and juries were less likely to convict solely on statements. Defendants have the right to produce evidence in their defense and examine evidence held by the opposing party or the court.

The rate of acquittals and cases withdrawn by the prosecution due to insufficient evidence continued to be high, particularly for sexual offenses, murder, and gang-related cases. These actions were often due to failure of witnesses to testify because of fear for life and personal safety.

Political Prisoners and Detainees

There were no reports of political prisoners or detainees.

Civil Judicial Procedures and Remedies

Persons have the right to bring legal actions for alleged violations of rights protected under the constitution regardless of whether there is also implementing legislation. The Supreme Court hears most civil suits, but the magistrate's courts have jurisdiction over civil cases involving sums of less than 5,000 Belize dollars (BZ$) ($2,500). In addition to civil cases, the Supreme Court has jurisdiction over cases involving human rights issues. The backlog of civil cases in the Supreme Court continued to be significant; 806 cases were filed in 2015. Mediation as an alternative method to settle disputes became part of the legal system in 2013, and judges have referred 115 cases for mediation since its inception in 2013. The National Mediation Committee was tasked with extending mediation to the magistrate's and family courts.

Litigants may appeal cases to the Caribbean Court of Justice, the country's highest appellate court.

Property Restitution

During the year the government settled compensation claims with two foreign-owned major utility companies that it nationalized: Belize Telecommunication Limited (BTL) in 2009 and Belize Electricity Limited in 2011. In September the judiciary ruled on the final payment the government owed to the previous owner of BTL; only half of the payment was made as of the end of October.

f. Arbitrary Interference with Privacy, Family, Home, or Correspondence

The constitution prohibits such actions, and government authorities generally respected these prohibitions.

Section 2. Respect for Civil Liberties, Including:

a. Freedom of Speech and Press

The law provides for freedom of speech and press, and the government generally respected these rights. An independent press, an effective judicial system, and a functioning democratic political system combined to promote freedom of speech and press.

In an August session of the House of Representatives, four police officers forcibly removed a news reporter, which raised concerns about the treatment of the media. Other journalists were forcibly pushed out of the media gallery, allegedly under instructions from the Speaker of the House of Representatives. Reporters claimed it was an attempt to censor their coverage of the actions of police inside the chamber (when an opposition representative was also forcibly removed).

Libel/Slander Laws: Independent groups noted some concerns with defamation suits. In July Secretary General Myrtle Palacio of the opposition People's United Party (PUP) sued the editor of the ruling UDP newspaper (*The Guardian*) for defamation of character after the newspaper published a cartoon depicting Palacio practicing and endorsing witchcraft. Palacio argued the cartoon was an attack on her reputation and her culture (Garifuna). The court sided with the newspaper's editor and ordered Palacio to pay the defendant's court costs of BZ$5,000 ($2,500).

Internet Freedom

The government did not restrict or disrupt access to the internet or censor online content, and there were no credible reports that the government monitored private online communications without appropriate legal authority. According to the Caribbean-based Broadband Commission for Digital Development, 20 percent of households were connected to broadband internet, but the telecommunication companies offering wireless internet service estimated that approximately 40 percent of the population had access to the internet by the end of 2015.

Academic Freedom and Cultural Events

There were no government restrictions on academic freedom or cultural events.

b. Freedom of Peaceful Assembly and Association

The law provides for freedom of assembly and association, and the government generally respected these rights.

c. Freedom of Religion

See the Department of State's *International Religious Freedom Report* at www.state.gov/religiousfreedomreport/.

d. Freedom of Movement, Internally Displaced Persons, Protection of Refugees, and Stateless Persons

The constitution provides for freedom of internal movement, foreign travel, emigration, and repatriation, and the government generally respected these rights. After a nearly 20-year hiatus in accepting refugee claims, the government reconstituted its Refugee Eligibility Committee in November 2015 and reestablished its Refugee Department in March 2016. Prior to the establishment of the Refugee Department, the Immigration and Nationality Department handled individual cases but did not make any determinations on asylum claims in nearly 20 years. The UN High Commissioner for Refugees (UNHCR) reactivated its presence in Belize in October 2015. Although the government committed to provide protection and assistance to refugees, asylum seekers, persons at risk of becoming stateless, or other persons of concern under the UN Convention on the Status of Refugees, the Belize Refugees Act, and the UN Convention for Statelessness, the government has yet to take action to meet the needs of these new cases.

In-country Movement: In April to defuse cross-border tensions and to ensure public safety, the government introduced a statutory instrument temporarily prohibiting citizens from accessing the Sarstoon River for 30 days. The statutory instrument's constitutionality was widely questioned, and it was lifted four days before it was set to expire due to public pressure.

Protection of Refugees

<u>Access to Asylum</u>: The law provides for the granting of asylum or refugee status within 14 days, but of the more than 70 cases reviewed by the Refugee Eligibility Committee since the committee was reconstituted in November 2015, the government has not granted asylum status to anyone. The nongovernmental organization (NGO) Help for Progress, UNHCR's implementing partner in the country, continued to assist with UNHCR's persons of concern.

An increasing number of persons from Central America, particularly El Salvador, sought protection in Belize. As of December the Refugee Department received 1,400 asylum applications, although there were separate reports that approximately 3,000 applications were filed. In November 2015 the reactivated Refugee Eligibility Committee, responsible for reviewing refugee applications, met for the first time in 18 years. Moreover, the passports of those applying for asylum who did not meet the government's 14-day deadline were unable to work legally in the country and their passports were stamped with a "Refugee Department" stamp. UNHCR recommended the government eliminate the use of stamps indicating the status of refugees or asylum seekers on passports. While the government stopped stamping passports for refugees, it continued the practice for asylum seekers.

<u>Employment</u>: Persons awaiting adjudication of their asylum cases and not meeting the government's 14-day deadline were unable to work legally in the country.

<u>Durable Solutions</u>: When the refugee status of an asylum seeker is confirmed, refugees may be issued permanent residency with the possibility of obtaining citizenship after extensive stays.

<u>Temporary Protection</u>: The Immigration Department issued renewable special residency permits for periods of 60 to 90 days to asylum seekers who met the 14-day deadline.

Section 3. Freedom to Participate in the Political Process

The constitution provides citizens the ability to choose their government through free and fair periodic elections held by secret ballot and based on universal and equal suffrage.

Elections and Political Participation

<u>Recent Elections</u>: In November 2015 the UDP won 19 seats in the 31-seat National Assembly, equaling the majority with which it entered the election. The OAS observation team reported generally free and fair elections. The elected candidates in general represented a cross section of the races and cultures present in the country.

<u>Participation of Women and Minorities</u>: No laws limit the participation of women and minorities in the political process, but observers suggested cultural and societal constraints limited the number of women participating in government. While women remained a clear minority in government, both major parties declared they took steps to increase female participation. During the November 2015 general elections, 11 women ran for office and two were elected to the House of Representatives. The UDP appointed two women to the 12-person Senate, and the opposition PUP appointed one. For the first time, a woman was appointed to the position of attorney general. During the year the government named two of the female senators as ministers.

Section 4. Corruption and Lack of Transparency in Government

The law provides criminal penalties for corruption by officials, but the government did not implement the law effectively, and officials sometimes engaged in corrupt practices. The World Bank's worldwide governance indicators reflected that corruption continued to be a problem.

<u>Corruption</u>: Allegations of corruption in government among public officials, including ministers and chief executive officers, were numerous, although no substantial proof was presented in most cases. In August, three special reports by the auditor general regarding immigration irregularities between 2011 and 2013 named at least 12 former and sitting cabinet ministers as allegedly "interfering" with the issuance of visas, nationality, and passports. Authorities agreed to calls by the opposition and civil society to form a Senate inquiry to investigate corruption in the Immigration and Nationality Department in light of the auditor general's reports.

Although the Ombudsman's Office reported fewer official complaints than in previous years, citizens continued to allege corruption against the Lands Department for illegally distributing lands to party associates. Despite accusations of political cronyism, the government insisted that it maintained transparency in the distribution of land.

In October former deputy prime minister Gaspar Vega resigned as cabinet minister following a revelation that his son, Andre Vega, had benefited from an illegal land transaction during the elder Vega's tenure as minister responsible for land distribution. In 2014 the government gave the title for a piece of land that already had an owner to Andre Vega. Documents from the Lands Department indicated that the ministry was warned that the property was privately owned already, but a title was still issued to one of Minister Vega's close advisors for BZ$2,500 ($1,250), who in turn sold it to the minister's son for BZ$15,000 ($7,500). When the Land Department noticed the "discrepancy," Andre Vega was compensated at market value because the government had given him a title to land already owned. The compensation was valued at BZ$400,000 ($200,000).

Financial Disclosure: The law requires public officials to submit annual financial disclosure statements, which the Integrity Commission reviews. At the same time, the constitution allows authorities to prohibit citizens from questioning the validity of such statements. Anyone who does so, either orally or in writing, outside a rigidly prescribed procedure is subject to a fine of up to BZ$5,000 ($2,500), three years' imprisonment, or both. The Integrity Commission had been dormant for most of its existence since 1994 and last functioned in 2014. In September, 11 opposition members of parliament filed their earnings and assets and called for members of the ruling party to follow. On November 30, after public demonstrations urging good governance measures, the prime minister, with the concurrence of the leader of the opposition appointed seven members to the Integrity Commission who should serve until the end of 2018.

Public Access to Information: The law provides for public access to documents of a ministry or prescribed authority upon written request, although it protects a number of categories, such as documents from the courts or those related to national security, defense, or foreign relations. The government must supply to the Office of the Ombudsman a written reason for any denial of access, the name of the person making the decision, and information on the right to appeal.

There were two cases in which government agencies denied freedom of information requests. Both cases were reported to the Office of the Ombudsman and later resolved.

Section 5. Governmental Attitude Regarding International and Nongovernmental Investigation of Alleged Violations of Human Rights

A variety of domestic and international human rights groups generally operated without government restriction, investigating and publishing their findings on human rights cases. Government officials often were cooperative and responsive to their views.

Government Human Rights Bodies: The ombudsman, although appointed by the government, acts as an independent check on governmental abuses. The Office of the Ombudsman holds a range of procedural and investigative powers, including the right to enter any premise to gather documentation and the right to summon persons. The office operated under significant staffing and financial constraints. The law requires the ombudsman to submit annual reports, and the office also created a midyear report to address problem trends. The office does not have the power to investigate allegations against the judiciary.

While the Ombudsman's Office technically has wide investigative powers, noncompliance from the offices it investigates severely limited its effectiveness. Through 2015 only 35 percent of complaints to the office had been resolved or were under investigation; 6.4 percent were resolved by other means (mediation outside the Ombudsman's Office), and 58.5 percent remained unresolved. The backlog continued to grow.

The Human Rights Commission, an independent, volunteer-based government agency, continued to operate, but only on an ad hoc basis, constrained by funding and staffing limitations. Nevertheless, NGOs and other organizations stated the Human Rights Commission was more active and vocal than in previous years. The commission provided human rights training for police recruits, prison officers, and the BDF.

Section 6. Discrimination, Societal Abuses, and Trafficking in Persons

Women

Rape and Domestic Violence: The criminal code criminalizes rape, including spousal rape. The code states that a person convicted of rape or marital rape shall be sentenced to imprisonment for eight years to life, although sentences were sometimes much lighter. Challenges to the wider justice system generally resulted in poor conviction rates for rape offenses. A number of cases resulted in acquittals or discontinuance because the accusing party dropped the charges or refused to testify at trial. In many instances the failure to proceed with a case was due to the victim's fear for personal safety. Perceived inefficiencies in the police and judicial systems as well as fear of further violence, retribution, and social stigma contributed to the underreporting of rapes.

Domestic violence was frequently prosecuted with charges such as "harm," "wounding," "grievous harm," rape, and marital rape but were treated as civil matters. Police, prosecutors, and judges recognized both physical violence and mental injury. Penalties include fines or imprisonment for violations; the level of fine or length of sentence depends on the severity of the crime. The law empowers the Family Court to issue protection orders against accused offenders. Persons who may apply for protection orders against domestic violence include de facto spouses or persons in "visiting relations," defined as couples in a relationship but not living together. Protection orders may remain in place for up to three years and may include a requirement for child support where applicable.

There were 15 cases of gender-based murder against women. In March the mother of seven children was stabbed to death by her common-law husband. In July another woman, a mother of three, was killed while socializing with a group of men. In September a pregnant mother of two was shot and killed inside her house in front of her children.

The Women's Department under the Ministry of Human Development and Social Transformation and the first lady and special envoy for women and children continued their campaign against gender-based and domestic violence. The Women's Department received referrals from both the criminal and civil courts. The BPD operated a toll-free domestic violence hotline, and most of the major police stations in the country had designated domestic abuse offices administered by a female police officer where victims could make their complaints. A lack of resources and coordination among the response agencies inhibited the provision of viable alternatives for victims.

Three women's shelters in the country offered short-term housing but lacked the resources and staff to provide other basic services to victims of domestic violence. By mid-year resource shortages led to the closing of one of the shelters. There were no transitional or medium-term shelters to assist victims to move toward independent living.

<u>Sexual Harassment</u>: The law provides protection from sexual harassment in the workplace, including provisions against unfair dismissal of a victim of sexual harassment in the workplace. The Women's Department recognizes sexual harassment as a subset of sexual violence.

Many cases of sexual harassment allegedly went unreported. There were several anecdotal reports that female officers in the police and defense force were victims of sexual abuse. In October, two female police officers attached to the Gang Suppression Unit reported to the Office of the Ombudsman sexually assaults by their male colleagues. The matter was under investigation both internally and by the ombudsman.

Reproductive Rights: Couples and individuals have the right to decide the number, spacing, and timing of their children; manage their reproductive health; and have access to the information and means to do so, free from discrimination, coercion, or violence.

Discrimination: The law provides for the same legal status and rights for women as for men. The law also mandates equal pay for equal work and was generally respected. The law provides generally for the continuity of employment and protection against unfair dismissal, including for sexual harassment in the work place, pregnancy, or HIV status.

The BDF and Belize Coast Guard maintain a 5 percent and 10 percent cap respectively for female service members.

Despite legal provisions for gender equality and government programs aimed at empowering women, NGOs and other observers reported women faced social and economic discrimination. Although participating in all spheres of national life and outnumbering men in university classrooms and in high school graduation rates, women held relatively few top managerial positions. The labor commissioner verified that men traditionally earned more--on average BZ$90 ($45) more per month than women--because they held higher managerial positions.

Children

Birth Registration: Citizenship is derived by birth within the country's territory, regardless of the nationality of the parents. Citizenship may also be acquired by descent if at least one parent is a citizen of the country. The standard provision is for births to be registered no later than a week after birth; registration after a month is considered late and includes a minimal fine. The Vital Statistical Office and the Ministry of Health have an agreement to offer bedside registration in hospitals shortly after birth.

<u>Education</u>: Primary education is free, and education is compulsory between the ages of six and 14; however, primary schools may incorporate other fees, and parents may be required to pay for textbooks, uniforms, and meals.

Through monthly payments the government assisted families of needy children at the primary school level and, to a limited extent, the secondary school level. The Ministry of Education continued to assist secondary school students in the two southern districts with a grant of BZ$300 ($150) for two years of high school. Students in other parts of the country had to apply to qualify for the subsidy.

<u>Child Abuse</u>: Abuse of children occurred, and as of the end of October, 1,217 cases were reported to authorities.

Sexual intercourse with a girl under age 14 is an offense punishable by 12 years to life imprisonment. Unlawful sexual intercourse with a girl ages 14-16 is an offense punishable by five to 10 years' imprisonment.

In September, David Taylor was convicted of committing extreme acts of pornographic exploitation of three boys in 2012. After three years in trial, Taylor pleaded guilty to three counts of indecent assault.

In July the commander of the Gang Suppression Unit, Mark Flowers, was placed on interdiction after a minor reported that Flowers had unlawful sexual intercourse with her on two occasions. The minor, who was 14 years old, was five months pregnant when she made the report. The matter awaited trial at year's end.

The law allows authorities to remove a child from an abusive home environment and requires parents to maintain and support children until the age of 18. There were publicized cases of underage girls' being victims of sexual abuse and mistreatment, in most cases in their own home or in the home of a relative.

The Family Services Division in the Ministry of Human Development and Social Transformation is the government office with the lead responsibility for children's problems. The division coordinated programs for children who were victims of domestic violence, advocated remedies in specific cases before the Family Court, conducted public education campaigns, investigated cases of trafficking in children, and worked with local and international NGOs and the UN Children's Fund (UNICEF) to promote children's welfare.

Early and Forced Marriage: The legal minimum age to marry is 18, but persons between ages 16 and 18 may marry with the consent of parents, legal guardians, or judicial authority. According to UNICEF 26 percent of women ages 20 to 24 were married or cohabitating before age 18.

Sexual Exploitation of Children: The law establishes penalties for child prostitution, child pornography, child sexual exploitation, and indecent exhibition of a child. It defines a "child" as anyone under age 18. The law stipulates that the offense of child prostitution does not apply to persons exploiting 16- and 17-year-old children in sexual activity in exchange for remuneration, gifts, goods, food, or other benefits. NGOs expressed concern that this specific clause in the law could render children vulnerable to commercial sexual exploitation, including sex trafficking, due to the common practice of parents' pushing their children to provide sexual favors to older men in exchange for remuneration. The legal age for consensual sex is 16, but prostitution is not legal under 18.

There were anecdotal reports that boys and girls were exploited in child prostitution, including the "sugar daddy" syndrome whereby older men provided money to young women and/or their families for sexual relations. Similarly, there were reports of increasing exploitation of minors, often to meet the demand of foreign sex tourists in tourist-populated areas or where there were transient and seasonal workers. The law criminalizes the procurement or attempted procurement of "a person" under age 18 to engage in prostitution; an offender is liable to eight years' imprisonment. The government did not effectively enforce laws prohibiting child sex trafficking.

The law establishes a penalty of two years' imprisonment for persons convicted of publishing or offering for sale any obscene book, writing, or representation.

International Child Abductions: The country is a party to the 1980 Hague Convention on the Civil Aspects of International Child Abduction. For information see the Department of State's *Annual Report on International Parental Child Abduction* at travel.state.gov/content/childabduction/en/legal/compliance.html.

Anti-Semitism

The Jewish population was small, and there were no reports of anti-Semitic acts.

Trafficking in Persons

See the Department of State's *Trafficking in Persons Report* at
www.state.gov/j/tip/rls/tiprpt/.

Persons with Disabilities

The law does not expressly prohibit discrimination against persons with physical, sensory, intellectual, and mental disabilities in employment, education, air or other transportation, access to health care, or the provision of other government services. The constitution provides for the protection of all citizens from any type of discrimination. The law does not provide for accessibility to persons with disabilities, and most public and private buildings and transportation were not accessible to them. Certain businesses, such as banks and government departments (social security offices), had designated clerks to attend to the elderly and persons with disabilities. There were no policies to encourage hiring of persons with disabilities in the private or public sectors.

Mental health provisions and protections generally were poor. Informal government-organized committees for persons with disabilities were tasked with public education and advocating for protections against discrimination. Private companies and NGOs provided services to persons with disabilities. The Ministry of Education maintained an educational unit offering limited special education programs within the regular school system. There were two schools and four special education centers for children with disabilities.

In June a schizophrenic man attacked three adults and three minors with a machete, fatally injuring one of the minors. Police detained the attacker and held him in the Belize Central Prison. He was charged with aggravated assault and murder and scheduled to undergo an evaluation to determine his fitness to stand trial. A psychiatrist from the public health system said the man was placed at the prison because there was no other suitable place for him. Residents from his community petitioned police to have him moved from the prison for security reasons but the petition has not yet been heard.

The Special Envoy for Women and Children, Kim Simplis Barrow, spouse of the prime minister, continued advocacy campaigns on behalf of persons with disabilities, especially children, and supported efforts to promote schools that took steps to create inclusive environments for persons with disabilities.

Indigenous People

No separate legal system or laws cover indigenous persons, since the government maintains that it treats all citizens the same. Employers, public and private, generally treated indigenous persons equally with other ethnic groups for employment and other purposes.

The Maya Leaders' Alliance (MLA), composed of the Toledo Maya Council, Q'eche Council of Belize, Toledo Alcaldes Association, the Julian Cho Society, and the Tumul K'in Center of Learning, monitored development in the Toledo District with the goal of protecting Mayan land and culture. While the government noted the need to respect and consult the Mayan communities when issuing oil exploration licenses in the south, the alliance believed it was not consulted properly before decisions were taken. The government, without consulting the Mayan community, renewed a one-year extension contract for petroleum exploration for U.S. Capital Energy over which the Supreme Court had given the Mayan community some jurisdiction in a 2010 decision.

In January the government established the Maya Land Rights Commission to honor a Caribbean Court of Justice court order for the government to legitimize communal land rights for traditional Mayan villages. As of October, however, no progress was made, and the MLA claimed the government was deliberately stalling and not acting in good faith.

Acts of Violence, Discrimination, and Other Abuses Based on Sexual Orientation and Gender Identity

In July the Belize Supreme Court interpreted Section 53 of the criminal code that criminalized sexual acts "against the order of nature" to clarify that Section 53 does not apply to sexual acts between consenting adults in private.

In September the government partially appealed the ruling, conceding the decriminalization of homosexuality but questioning a section of the decision that made "sexual orientation" a protected class. The Roman Catholic Church and the National Evangelical Association of Belize submitted an appeal of the entire ruling.

The Immigration Act prohibits "homosexual" persons from entering the country, but immigration authorities did not enforce the law.

The extent of discrimination based on sexual orientation or gender identity was difficult to ascertain due to lack of official reporting. According to the NGO United Belize Advocacy Movement (UniBAM), 34 killings based on sexual orientation and gender identity had occurred since 1997. At the end of October, UniBAM had registered six cases of violence as a result of sexual orientation and gender identity, including cases involving homicide, violent attacks, (political) hate speech, medical service discrimination during pregnancy, denial of education due to sexual orientation and gender identity, and family-based violence.

As of October police made no arrests regarding the January 2015 killing of an openly gay man. The LGBTI community classified the killing as a hate crime, but the police did not declare it as such.

Local LGBTI rights advocates noted that, while LGBTI persons still feared police and were harassed or intimidated while reporting crimes, police relations slightly improved. UniBAM reported that continuing harassment and insults by the public affected its activities and that its members were reluctant to file complaints.

HIV and AIDS Social Stigma

There was some societal discrimination against persons with HIV/AIDS, and the government worked to combat it through public education efforts of the National AIDS Commission under the Ministry of Human Development. NGOs such as the Pan American Social Marketing Organization also actively countered discrimination against persons with HIV/AIDS. The law provides for protection of workers against unfair dismissal, including for HIV status.

Section 7. Worker Rights

a. Freedom of Association and the Right to Collective Bargaining

The law, including related regulations and statutes, generally provides for the right to establish and join independent trade unions, bargain collectively, and conduct legal strikes. The law also prohibits antiunion discrimination, dissolution, or suspension of unions by administrative authority. It requires reinstatement of workers fired for union activity. The Ministry of Labor, Local Government, and Rural Development (Ministry of Labor) recognizes unions and employers associations after they are registered, and the law establishes procedures for the registration and status of trade unions and employers organizations and for collective bargaining.

The law allows authorities to refer disputes involving public and private sector employees who provide "essential services" to compulsory arbitration, prohibit strikes, and terminate actions. The national fire service, postal service, monetary and financial services, civil aviation and airport security services, port authority personnel (stevedores and pilots), and security services are deemed essential services beyond the International Labor Organization definition of essential services.

Workers can file complaints with the Ministry of Labor or seek redress from the courts, although it remained difficult to prove that terminations were due to union activity. The department generally handled labor cases without lengthy delays and dealt with appeals via arbitration outside of the court system. The court did not apply the law requiring reinstatement of workers fired for union activity and provided monetary compensation instead.

There was a lack of resources to carry out the mandate of the ministry's Labor Department, including a shortage of vehicles and fuel to ensure compliance, particularly in rural areas. There were no complaints of administrative or judicial delays relating to labor complaints and disputes, although in the past labor disputes took an extended time to resolve through the court system. Information on penalties for violations of freedom of association or collective bargaining was unavailable.

The government and employers did not always effectively enforce the law. Antiunion discrimination and other forms of employer interference in union functions sometimes occurred, and on several occasions unions threatened or carried out strikes. In September the Belize National Teacher's Union (BNTU) pressured the government to address national problems, particularly corruption by public officers. The teachers held a national strike, shutting down schools once in August and once in October. The prime minister pleaded for the BNTU membership to cancel the strike. Authorities threatened not to pay teachers on the days they strike and to pass a law allowing the government to hire temporary teachers to replace those on strike. Help for Progress continued to petition the Inter-American Commission on Human Rights to highlight, among other things, concerns with employers' measures that do not allow migrant workers to unionize and that require migrants to submit to HIV tests in certain industries. The NGO stated that in certain industries, particularly the banana, citrus, and construction industries, employers often did not respect due process, did not pay minimum wages, and classified workers as contract and nonpermanent employees to avoid providing certain benefits. The NGO noted that both national and migrant workers were denied rights and that the Labor Department was inadequately staffed and under resourced.

b. Prohibition of Forced or Compulsory Labor

The constitution prohibits all forms of forced or compulsory labor. Penalties for forced or compulsory labor are covered under the anti-trafficking law and carry prison sentences of one to eight years for adult victims and one to 12 years for child victims, which were comparable to penalties for other major offenses and sufficient to deter violations, although the government did not enforce this law. Resources and inspections to deter violations were limited. The government did not identify any forced labor victims during the year.

Forced labor of both Belizean and foreign women occurred in bars, nightclubs, and domestic service. Migrant men, women, and children were at risk for forced labor in agriculture, fishing, and in the service sector, including restaurants and shops, particularly among the South Asian and Chinese communities.

Also see the Department of State's *Trafficking in Persons Report* at www.state.gov/j/tip/rls/tiprpt/.

c. Prohibition of Child Labor and Minimum Age for Employment

The law prohibits the employment of children under age 14 in industrial jobs and shop work, but not for all sectors. Light work is allowed for children ages 12 to 13. Children ages 14 to 18 may be employed only in an occupation that a labor officer has determined is "not injurious to the moral or physical development of nonadults." Children under age 16 are excluded from work in factories, and those under age 18 are excluded from working at night or in certain kinds of employment deemed dangerous. For guidance the Labor Department used a list of dangerous occupations for young workers, but the list has not been adopted as law.

The law permits children to work on family farms and in family-run businesses. National legislation does not address a situation in which child labor is contracted between a parent and the employer. The National Child Labor Policy distinguishes between children engaged in work that is beneficial to their development and those engaged in the worst forms of child labor. The policy identifies children involved in the worst forms of child labor as those engaged in hazardous work, trafficking and child slavery, commercial sexual activities, and illicit activities.

The Labor Department has primary responsibility for implementing labor policies and enforcing labor laws, but it had limited dedicated resources to investigate complaints. Inspectors from the Labor and Education Departments are responsible for enforcing these regulations. The penalty for employing a child below minimum age is a fine not exceeding BZ$20 ($10) or imprisonment not exceeding two months. On a second offense, the law stipulates a fine not exceeding BZ$50 ($25) or imprisonment not exceeding four months. There was not enough information provided to determine if the penalties, remediation, and inspections were sufficient to deter violations. There was no information on whether child labor laws were well enforced. There is also a National Child Labor Committee under the National Committee for Families and Children, a statutory interagency group that advocates for policies and legislation to protect children and eliminate child labor.

Some children were vulnerable to forced labor, particularly in the agriculture, fishing, and service sectors. Commercial sexual exploitation of children occurred (see section 6, Children). According to the Statistical Institute of Belize, the country's child labor rate was 3.7 percent, with the problem most prevalent in rural areas; 74 percent of children illegally employed were boys.

Also see the Department of Labor's *Findings on the Worst Forms of Child Labor* at www.dol.gov/ilab/reports/child-labor/findings/.

d. Discrimination with Respect to Employment and Occupation

The law and regulations prohibit discrimination on the basis of race, sex, gender, language, HIV-positive status or other communicable diseases, or social status. The government did not effectively enforce those laws and regulations. The law does not explicitly prohibit discrimination in employment with respect to disability or to sexual or orientation and/or gender identity. There were reports that discrimination in employment and occupation occurred with respect to sexual orientation. One NGO reported that members of the LGBTI community often had problems gaining and retaining employment due to discrimination in the workplace, but these claims were not verified. There were no officially reported cases of discrimination at work based on ethnicity, culture, or skin color; although anecdotal evidence suggested that such cases occurred.

e. Acceptable Conditions of Work

The national minimum wage was BZ$3.30 ($1.65) per hour. A full-time worker receiving the minimum wage earned between 1.5 to two times the poverty limit income, depending on the district. The law sets the workweek at no more than six days or 45 hours and requires premium payment for overtime work. Workers are entitled to two workweeks' paid annual holiday. Additionally there are 13 days designated as public and bank holidays. Employees who work on public and bank holidays are entitled to pay at time-and-a-half, except for Good Friday and Christmas, which are paid at twice the normal rate.

Several different health and safety regulations cover numerous industries. The law, which applies to all sectors, prescribes that the employer must take "reasonable care" for the safety of employees in the course of their employment. The law further states that every employer who provides or arranges accommodation for workers to reside at or in the vicinity of a place of employment shall provide and maintain sufficient and hygienic housing accommodations, a sufficient supply of wholesome water, and sufficient and proper sanitary arrangements.

The Ministry of Labor did not always effectively enforce minimum wage and health and safety regulations. The ministry's Labor Department had 25 labor officers in 10 offices throughout the country. Inspections were not sufficient to secure compliance, especially in the more remote areas. Fines varied according to the infraction but generally were not very high and thus not sufficient to deter violations. Although several cases were pending, a labor tribunal had not been established since being created in 2011.

The minimum wage generally was respected. Nevertheless, anecdotal evidence from NGOs and employers suggested that undocumented Central American workers, particularly young service workers and agricultural laborers, were regularly paid below the minimum wage.

While no known reports were made to the Labor Department, several individuals appeared in the media alleging that in certain industries employers often did not respect due process, did not pay minimum wages, and classified workers as contract and nonpermanent employees to avoid certain benefits.

There was a fatal injury at Belize Sugar Industries when a mechanic was crushed by a heavy-duty machine. The company established an internal investigation with assistance from the BPD. The family of the victim received compensation because the employee was insured. There was also a fatal injury at Santander Sugar mill where a cane cutter ran over and killed an employee as he slept during his break. With the assistance of the BPD, an internal investigation was launched. There were no officially reported complaints of major industrial factory fires or mine disasters. It was unclear whether workers could remove themselves from situations that endangered health or safety without jeopardy to their employment or whether authorities effectively protected employees in this situation.